The *Amazing* 2000-Hour Flashlight

EXCELLENT FLASHLIGHT MODIFICATION BOOK :-)
This book will allow ANYONE to build a 2000 hour flashlight. The book is so detailed and well written that even "non-handy" folks can use it effectively. Thanks Mr. Brown! — *handyman166*

PERFECT
To Ron Brown: Thank you. Short, sweet and to the point . . . Seriously readable, too. This is the first How-To book I have ever read cover to cover and wanted more. — *Virginia Candela*

EASY . . . CONCISE.
Easily understood. Gives sources and part numbers. Can't ask for better. — *LucMee*

I DON'T HAVE TO RESEARCH THIS, RON DID IT FOR ME.
Thanks Ron. Great book and interesting experimentation to find the right combo. Saved me a lot of time. I hope you sell a million of these. — *Jim Caldwell*

THE AMAZING 2000-HOUR FLASHLIGHT
. . . definitely deserves some sort of consideration for perhaps the best use of $3 I can remember in a long time. — *Alex Smith*, author of *Home Remedies* [**NOTE:** $3 refers to the Kindle price for *Flashlights*, the only version available at the time.]

I HIGHLY RECOMMEND THIS E-BOOK
I have read through it and found that the materials are very easy to find, and the instructions are easy for me to figure out. — *Bernie Carr* (The Apartment Prepper's Blog) http://apartmentprepper.com/

The *Amazing* 2000-Hour Flashlight

Ron Brown

R&C Publishing

Newark Valley, New York

Notice: This manual is designed to provide information on flashlights.

It is not the purpose of this guide to reprint all the information that is otherwise available, but to complement, amplify, and supplement other texts and resources. You are urged to read all the available material and learn as much as you can about flashlights and to tailor the information to your specific circumstances.

Every effort has been made to make this guide as complete and accurate as possible. However, there may be mistakes, both typographical and in content. Therefore this text should be used only as a general guide and not as the ultimate source of flashlight modification. Furthermore, this guide contains information that is current only up to the printing date.

The purpose of this manual is to educate and entertain. The views, opinions, positions, of strategies expressed by the author are his alone. The author makes no representations as to the accuracy, completeness, correctness, suitability, or validity of any information in this book and will not be liable for any errors, omissions, or delays in this information or any losses, injuries, or damages arising from its use.

Disclosure: Several brand names are mentioned in this manual (Energizer, Walmart, Duracell, Eveready, etc.) but I receive no compensation in any form from any of them. In this manual I simply tell my story as I might tell a friend at the water cooler.

ISBN 978-0-9853337-2-0

Published by
R&C Publishing
15 Dr. Knapp Road South
Newark Valley, NY 13811

Printed in the United States of America

Table of Contents

Foreword

My interest in Prepping, or what I like to call modern survivalism, began when I moved to an island about 26 miles from the mainland of the United States. It did not take me long to realize that our little island paradise was dependent upon mainland suppliers for everything from food to fuel to basic electrical power. About the only thing we were blessed with was an abundant supply of water coming from our many lakes and aquifers.

In an effort to become self-reliant, I sought alternatives that would allow me to get by just fine, thank you very much, without dependence on others. High on the list was ensuring that I had adequate light. The Pacific Northwest can get pretty dark and gloomy.

Early on, I was lucky enough to hook up via email and the internet with Ron Brown and his book, *Lanterns, Lamps and Candles.* (Which, by the way, is an excellent primer on lighting for the do-it-yourselfer.) Later, when he asked if I was interested in a battery-operated flashlight that could run for 1000 hours on a single battery I said "heck yes".

And so began the many-month journey towards doing just that. Ron has put together some painstakingly detailed directions for building not just a 1000-hour flashlight but what has turned out to be a 2000-hour flashlight.

He shows you how to do this using simple materials and a nominal amount of skill. The 2000-hour flashlight can be built for less than $10, a trip to the local hardware store, and about half an hour of your time.

Why would you need such a long-lived flashlight? The answer is simple. Power outages. They can result from a storm, a hurricane, a tornado, or, as it happened in my area, someone hitting a transformer with their vehicle and blowing out the grid for three days. Beyond that, there is the possibility of a catastrophic electromagnetic pulse or EMP, that could throw the grid down for a week, a month, or even longer.

Having light to go about your day, to do your chores, to cook your food and to do a little bedtime reading are things we take for granted. Light is important. But more than that, an event that should represent a simple medical emergency — a tumble down the stairs or a baby who decides to be born at midnight — can, in darkness, blossom into a life-or-death crises. In such a circumstance, light is not just important; it is priceless.

To me, it is simply good common sense to have plenty of flashlights around. And here we have a 2000-hour flashlight. What more could you ask for?

Gaye Levy

❧✾☙❧✾☙

Want to learn more about basic preparedness? Please visit Gaye's website at www.backdoorsurvival.com where you will find tools for creating a self-reliant lifestyle through thoughtful prepping and optimism.

"Let there be light..." (Genesis 1:3)

IN THE BEGINNING... A Word About Batteries.

Flashlight batteries of the zinc-carbon type (General Purpose) and zinc-chloride (Heavy Duty) hark back to the World War II era. They are still made today.

Alkaline batteries, introduced in the 1960's, cost more and last longer.

All of these (zinc-carbon, zinc-chloride, and alkaline) are designed for one-time use. They are intended by their manufacturers to be disposable, not rechargeable.

Lithium batteries, introduced in the 1990's, raised the performance bar once again. Some lithium batteries are intended to be rechargeable; others, disposable.

Lithium is used as replacement chemistry in only the smaller battery sizes (button batteries, AAA, AA, and square 9-volt). Hence, lithium batteries have no bearing on the 2000-hour flashlight.

The purist might object to the way I've used the words "battery" and "cell" in this manual. I'm aware of the distinction but I've chosen to use the terms as they appear in everyday speech. Everyone says "flashlight batteries," for example, even though "cells" would be technically correct.

The 2000-Hour Flashlight. What Is It?

The 2000-hour flashlight uses big, square, 6-volt batteries of the alkaline persuasion. As its name implies, it produces useful light for 2000 nonstop hours — equivalent to $5^1/_2$ hours every evening for a year.

A common two-cell flashlight, the kind we all grew up with in the kitchen drawer, has an incandescent bulb (not LED) and two Heavy Duty D-cells (not alkaline). It produces useful light for eight hours. Accidentally leaving it on overnight results in a dead flashlight come morning.

Eight hours is thus the benchmark for flashlight performance most of us have tucked away in our brains. That's why 2000 hours is slightly jaw-dropping.

And what is "useful light"? The formal standard will be defined in a moment. For now, please know that "useful light" is sufficient to cook supper, change a car tire, or milk the cows.

Where Can I Get One?
As of this writing you cannot buy a 2000-hour flashlight off the shelf but you can easily build one. The purpose of this manual is to show you how. It's a half-hour project and consists of adding a 30-cent resistor to a $5 flashlight. The brands and part numbers and where to buy them are all identified.

How Does It Work?
It's the resistor that does the doing. The resistor, wired into the light's circuitry, "resists" current flow and reduces light output. That means lower current draw and longer battery life. There's a practical limit, of course, on how big a resistor can be used. It comes down to defining "useful" light. And that circles us around, once again, to the "standard."

Who Needs It?
For sure a 2000-hour flashlight would be a blessing for people in high-rise apartments.

When I wrote the book *Lanterns, Lamps & Candles: A User's Guide*, I never came fully to grips with the issue of a power outage when living in a high-rise — toting fuel up mega flights of stairs when the elevators weren't working or storing fuel beforehand in a cramped apartment.

A 60-year-old friend of mine lives on the 12th floor of a high-rise. The snapshots below are from her balcony. A lot of people live in high-rises.

Consider, too, underground fallout shelters, the polar opposite of high-rises. People are known to go slightly bonkers if there's no light in a shelter. But ordinary flashlights soon run down and shelter residents must choose between oxygen to breathe and oxygen to burn a candle.

The 2000-hour flashlight doesn't use any oxygen. How long will you stay in your shelter? Two weeks? This flashlight runs 12 weeks.

For sheer economy of operation, there's been nothing cheaper (till now) than a miniature kerosene "boudoir lamp" (the kind with the round, $1/8$" diameter wicks). Homemade knock-offs are used around the world because one-third cup of kerosene produces a candle-sized flame for 15 hours. At USA prices, that's half a cent per hour.

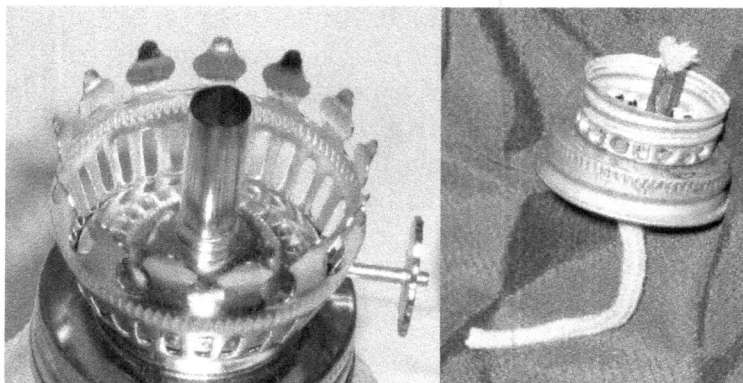

But the boudoir lamp has been trumped. The operating cost of the 2000-hour flashlight is 40% less than the cost of a kerosene boudoir lamp.

Safety considerations also favor the flashlight. All fire hazards are removed — in the barn with chaff and hay, around children and invalids where it might get knocked over, when fate has been unkind and you find yourself living in your car, or when checking out a potential gas leak after a natural disaster. Not to mention it smells a lot better than kerosene.

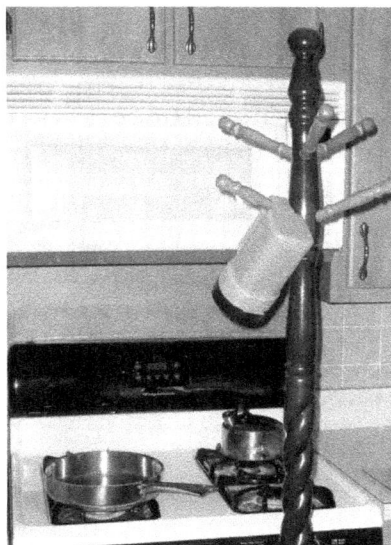

Giving Credit Where Credit Is Due

For me, the notion of adding a resistor to a flashlight came from a fellow named Luxstar (www.instructables.com/member/luxstar/). He shows how to build a 360-hour flashlight by soldering a resistor into a flashlight's circuitry. Realistically, I'm sure the resistor idea didn't originate with Luxstar any more than it did with me.

Flashaholics, as they're called, use all manner of esoteric stuff to create high-performance flashlights — HID bulbs (high intensity discharge), LiFePO4 batteries, etc. If you Google "hacking flashlights" you'll unseal the magic portal to an alternate universe.

Luxstar soldered a 56-ohm resistor into an Eveready Model 5109LS flashlight but he didn't upgrade the battery. He used the Heavy Duty battery that came with the light. So two thoughts come to mind. What if we use a bigger resistor, say 150 ohms? And what if we use an alkaline battery? As it turns out, those two tweaks are all it takes to produce a 2000-hour flashlight.

The icing on the cake is the fact that we don't have to solder anything. We can use "wire glue" instead, a black glue that contains carbon and conducts electricity. Wire glue reduces this task from a techie project to Junior High School level.

Unfortunately, Luxstar's performance criteria leave something to be desired:

> "The test started on the morning of 10-26-12. I was expecting a 200 hour run time. After 15 days (360 hours). The flashlight still puts out a usable amount of light. I can still read with it without any problem. I also got the opinion of a fellow flashlight enthusiast who thinks the flashlight is still useful for its intended purpose which is for the user to be able to easily see their way around the house in the dark and be able to easily read. The flashlight is noticeably dimmer than it was at the beginning of the test so I would conclude that this is a 360 hour flashlight." [sic]

That's a rather ambiguous standard by which to compare other designs. We'll return to the issue of benchmarking in a moment. Right now, let's just cut to the chase and build one of these things.

Bill of Materials

• Below. An Eveready 5109LS flashlight. Sources are listed in Appendix I.

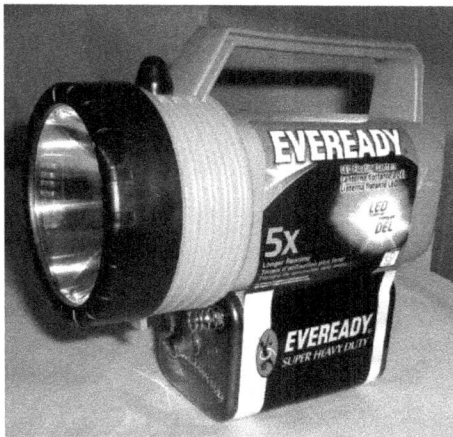

• Below. 150-ohm resistors. Radio Shack's price for a packet of five is $1.49 although you only need one. Radio Shack's Model No. and Catalog No. are the same: 2711109. Alternate sources are shown in Appendix I.

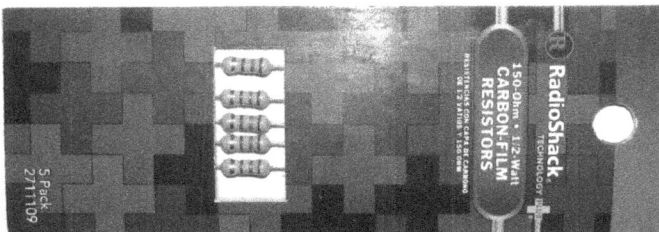

Below. Conductive wire glue. The Radio Shack part number is 6400146. Radio Shack's price is $5.49 for 0.3 fluid oz. Again, alternate sources are shown in Appendix I.

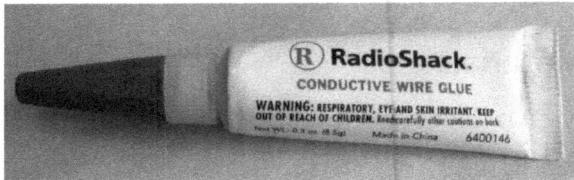

Tools

- needle-nose pliers
- small sidecutters (pliers) or nail clips
- $^1/_{16}$" drill bit or small nail

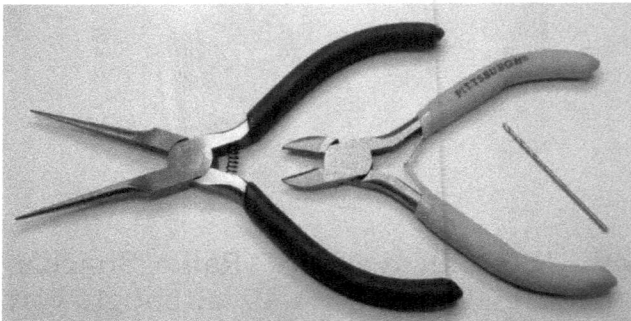

The Hack: How to Do the Modification

Step 1

Unscrew the front of the flashlight as if changing the battery. See below. The yellow body (the part that holds the battery), the black collar, and the clear plastic lens can be laid to one side. The bulb assembly is what we'll work on.

Step 2

Below, there are two (red) wires on the bulb assembly. We need to cut one of those wires in half so we can insert our resistor into the circuit. If wire cutters are lacking, nail clips can be used for the cutting. Cut the wire in the middle, leaving an equal amount of wire on each side.

Step 3

Next we need to strip the red insulation off the wire ends. We gently but firmly pull on the red insulation. It slides off end-ways. See below.

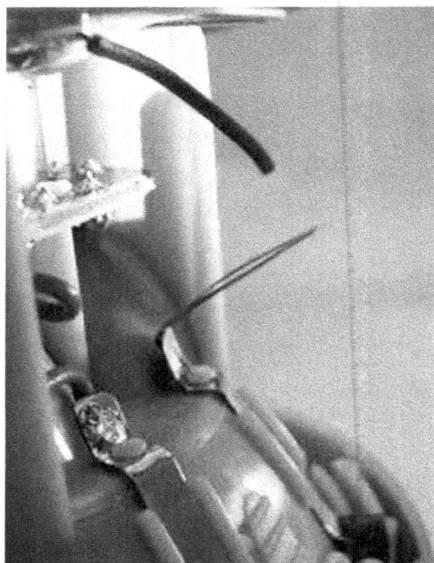

Step 4

Below, wrap one of the resistor wires around and around the shank of a $^1/_{16}$" drill bit. It will make about three wraps. Repeat the process with the other resistor leg.

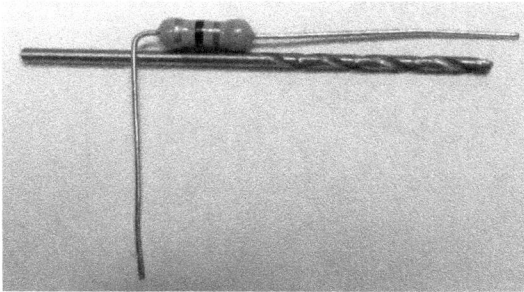

Step 5

Let's first do the end of the flashlight wire that attaches to the light's flat metal ring; that's the end that seems to give the most trouble. Thread the braided flashlight wire through the throat of the "coil spring" in the resistor wire.

Step 6

With pliers, crush flat the coil spring, trapping the braided flashlight wire inside. Then repeat Step #5 for the other end of the flashlight wire and flatten that end as well. At this point we should have solid mechanical connections (see below).

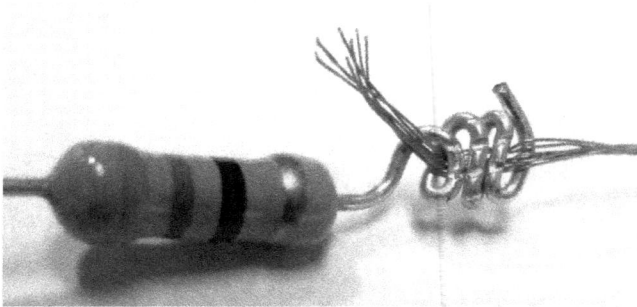

Step 7

Apply a drop of black wire glue to the joints just formed. The glue is runny stuff so insert a one-inch-wide strip of paper under the wires to shield other components. Be thrifty with the glue. More is not better.

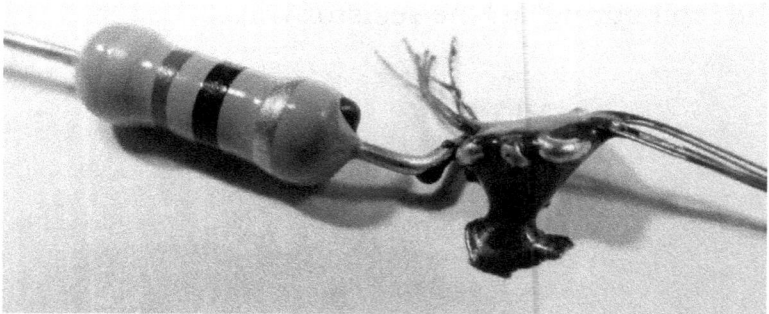

Step 8

After 15 or 20 minutes of drying, the glue will start to harden and you can remove the paper. At this point you can also snip off straggly wire ends. See below. Wow! Sure is purty, ain't it?

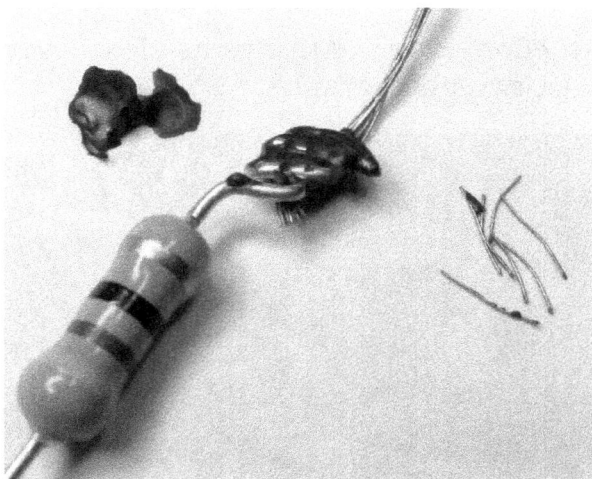

If you leave the paper in the bulb assembly overnight (instead of removing it when the glue becomes tacky) it may become firmly glued in place and need to be cut out with a razor blade.

Step 9

The glue needs to dry overnight at room temperature. After that, we can insert a battery into the body of the flashlight, add the newly modified bulb assembly, and screw on the collar/lens assembly. We can bend the resistor wires if necessary for clearance but everything the wires touch will be plastic so they don't need to be wrapped or otherwise shielded. *Voila!* A 2000-hour flashlight!

Final Assembly

Judging from reader feedback, nine out of ten people find the instructions in Steps #1-9, above, to be sufficient. But not everyone agrees. Some say "the directions lack clarity at the . . . [final] step where you add a resistor to your flashlight."

In an effort to make things as clear as possible I've added two photographs:

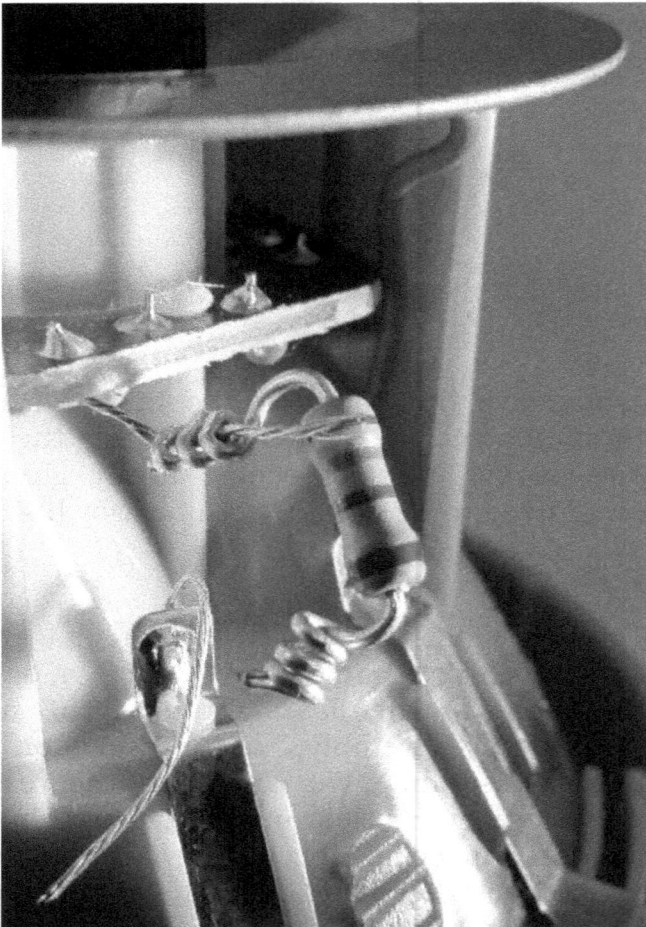

The photo above shows a stripped wire (see Step #3) threaded through the throat of the "spring" we created on one end of the resistor. The spring has been crimped (crushed flat) with pliers.

The crimping is important so that wire-end #1 doesn't decide of its own free will to escape from its spring-prison while you are busy with wire-end #2. These wires sometimes have a mind of their own.

The second photo, below, shows the second wire threaded through the throat of the second spring. As shown, the spring has not yet been crimped shut. That comes next.

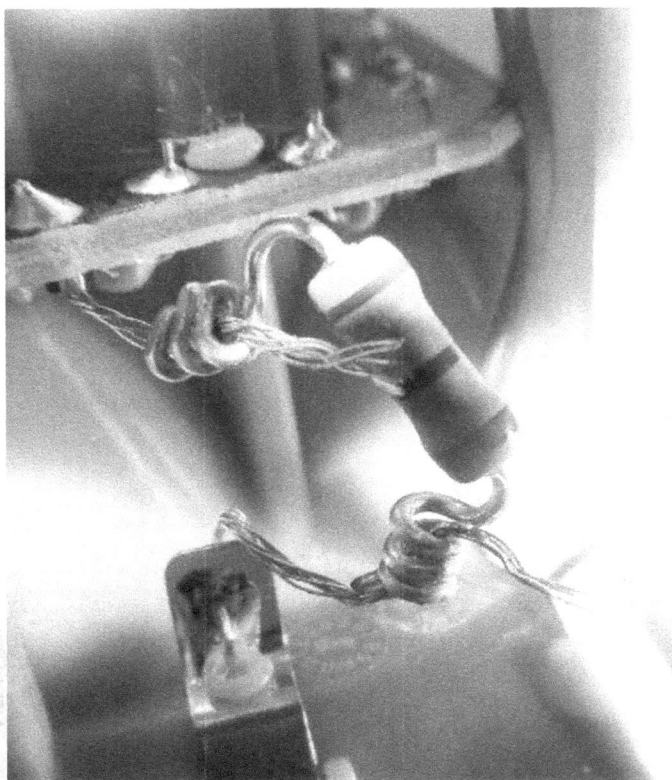

After that, wire glue is applied to both joints (springs) and the straggly braided wire ends trimmed or snipped off. With luck, this clarifies the assembly process.

A Variation for When You Get in Trouble

Due to clearance (or lack thereof) the wire end attached to the flashlight's flat metal ring can be difficult to join to the resistor wire. AND the braided flashlight wires are somewhat fragile. One fellow I know broke off the braided wire attached to the metal ring. His solution was to drill a hole in the ring and use a screw to secure that end of the resistor wire. It worked well.

If we use his method, we need to drill a hole. To do that, we must first make a dimple in the metal ring where the hole is to be. Below we see a small block of wood clamped in a vise, backing up the metal ring. A paneling nail has been used as a center punch to dimple the ring.

Drilling comes next. Use a $^5/_{64}$" drill bit.

I strongly urge you to employ a hand drill if at all possible (the old eggbeater kind). With an electric drill, the bit, at the precise instant it breaks through the metal, can snag on the metal being drilled and yank the flashlight assembly out of your hands, twirling it around at a frightening rate of speed.

Don't let it happen. Go slow. Wear gloves. Wear goggles. Think safety.

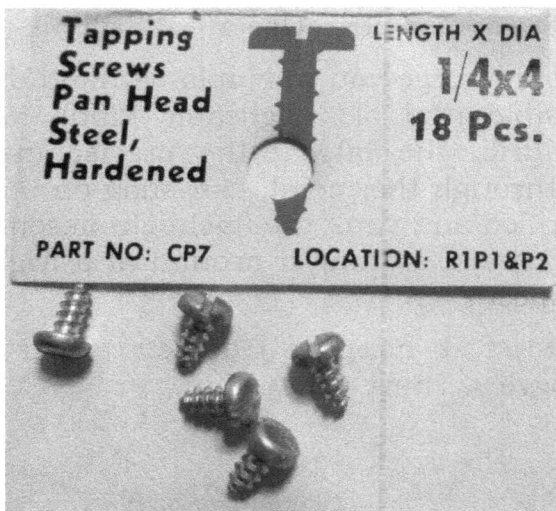

Tapping Screws
Pan Head
Steel,
Hardened

LENGTH X DIA
1/4x4
18 Pcs.

PART NO: CP7   LOCATION: R1P1&P2

The screws (above) are tiny, $1/4$" long. Shown below is a resistor wire trapped beneath a screw. The screw can be located anywhere on the ring as long as the end of the other braided flashlight wire is within reach. The screw head does not interfere with the battery terminal which is merely a spring resting on the flat ring.

Standard of Comparison

The stock 5109LS, as it comes from the store, produces 25 lumens. To be honest, when I first added a 150-ohm resistor, I was concerned whether or not the flashlight would produce sufficient illumination to be useful.

The Rayovac Model BRSGELI2AA-BA is a 5-lumen light with an LED bulb. It is pictured below.

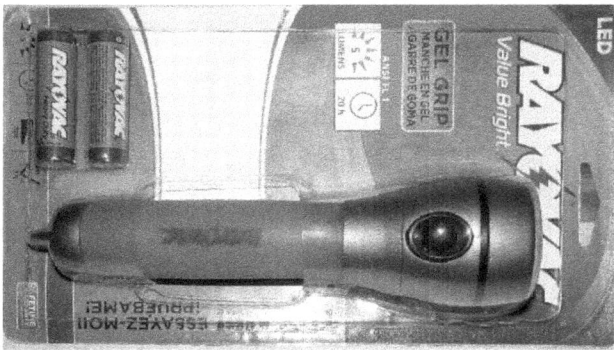

The 2000-hour flashlight (that is, an Eveready 5109LS with a 150-ohm resistor) produces slightly more light than this Rayovac. Consequently, I estimate the brightness of the 2000-hour light as 6 or 7 lumens. Stunning? No. Useful? Yes.

Now comes the hard part, the question of what to use as a cutoff point, a minimum, a threshold, to say that the 2000-hour light is NOT useful anymore? Here's where it gets sticky.

Flashlights are commonly rated in "lumens" and most lights provide that info on the label. The Eveready 5109LS does not. Online, however, various sellers (e.g. Best Buy, Walmart) state that the 5109LS outputs 25 lumens.

What the 5109LS wrapper does display is a little clock icon that says "FL 1 Standard 65h" (meaning 65 hours). "FL 1" stands for ANSI/NEMA FL 1 — Flashlight Basic Performance Standard. In that standard, run time is defined as "the continuous time lapsed from the initial light output to when the light is at 10% of the initial output."

So the FL 1 standard uses circular reasoning. A flashlight is measured in terms of itself. If the 5109LS starts out at 25 lumens, when it reaches 2.5 lumens its run time has expired. (According to Eveready, that's 65 hours.)

I would argue that we need a fixed standard of comparison, not a moving target. When I'm trying to compare light output and battery life using a 56-ohm resistor versus a 150-ohm resistor versus no resistor at all, a run-time benchmark defined as "10% of wherever you started" is pointless.

So I picked a light that supplies (in my opinion) a minimum threshold of useful light. It's the Maglite Solitaire. It's been around since 1988 and kicks out a blazing 2 lumens. Count 'em. Two.

Although the two-lumen Solitaire will not inspire Tarzan-yells and chest beating, it is undeniably useful; you'll be able to find your way to the privy at midnight. It's a practical standard by which to compare various flashlight designs. And it's widely available; Walmart carries it.

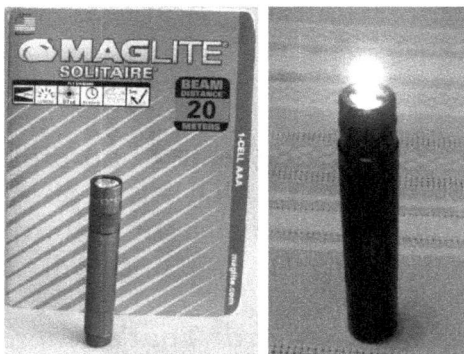

With the Solitaire, like every flashlight in the Maglite lineup, the lens cap and reflector can be removed and the light will continue burning — now a "candle" rather than a flashlight. But that means it can be used as a standard of comparison for battery-powered table lamps in addition to flashlights.

I bought a new Solitaire. The Solitaire's blister-pack contained a Duracell alkaline battery in addition to the flashlight. I swapped out the Duracell for a new Energizer Ultimate Lithium battery. I removed the lithium battery from the Solitaire between tests.

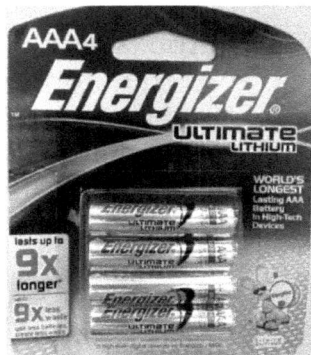

I used a pass/fail test to judge the modified 5109LS. As long as the flashlight being tested was visibly brighter than the brand new Solitaire, I judged the test-light as "passing." I would waggle my finger at the test-light and say, "Keep on trucking."

When the light being tested had dimmed to the point of being MERELY EQUAL to the brand new Solitaire, I judged the test-light to have "failed." I would then jerk my thumb and yell at the test-light, "You're outta here."

That was my standard. That's where the 2000 hours came from. You might well ask, of course, "How did you determine 'visibly brighter'?"

In answer, the simplest test I found was to stand in a dark room with the light being tested in one hand and the Solitaire (the control or standard) in the other and shine the lights in quick succession, one after the other, at an analog wall clock with a sweep second hand, twenty feet away. If you try it, you'll discover there really isn't much question about which one best illuminates the clock face.

Test Results

Given a standard, how do the lights compare?

• First, consider the stock 5109LS, equipped just as it comes from the store with an Eveready Heavy Duty battery and no added resistor. **For the first 200 hours it was brighter than a new Solitaire.** For the next 50 hours it was equal. After that, it gave off less light than a brand new Solitaire.

• Next we have Luxstar's 360-hour flashlight (so-called). It uses a 56-ohm resistor and an

Eveready Heavy Duty battery. **For the first 400 hours it was brighter than a new Solitaire.** For the next 100 hours it was equal.

• Last is our 2000-hour flashlight. It uses a 150-ohm resistor and (in this test) a Rayovac alkaline battery. **For the first 2000 hours it was brighter than a new Solitaire with a new lithium battery. For the next 500 hours it was equal.**

The Rayovac was the cheapest alkaline 6-volt I could find ($5.88 at Walmart). Duracell was 50% more ($8.87 at Lowe's).

In all these trials the flashlight being tested faded over time. The stock 5109LS, for example, did not run full speed ahead at 25 lumens for 200 hours and then suddenly collapse to two lumens. Rather, it faded slowly from beginning to end.

Recharging

Rechargeable 6-volt batteries with spring terminals are available but they are sealed lead-acid batteries rather than NiMH (nickel-metal hydride) or NiCd (nickel cadmium). They're used in game feeders of the type made by Moultrie and sold by Cabela's.

Let me quote the eBay sales pitch where I bought mine: "This 6V 5Ah UB650S Lantern is a sealed lead-acid (SLA) absorbed glass mat (AGM) rechargeable battery. AGM and GEL batteries are lead-acid and of the same battery chemistry (lead-oxide, lead sponge, and sulfuric acid electrolyte), but the electrolyte is stabilized differently. In AGM batteries, the electrolyte is suspended in fiberglass mat separators which act as absorbent sponges."

6V means 6-volt. 5Ah means 5 amp-hours. With shipping, rechargeable 6-volt batteries cost around $20. You need a battery with spring-type terminals (called "spring top" by the sellers).

Bright Mode versus Energy-Saver Mode

If bright light is preferred over long battery life, there's an easy way to bypass the resistor.

We need just one test lead, the kind with an alligator clip on each end. Attach alligator #1 to the north side of the resistor. Attach alligator #2

to the south side of the resistor. This provides an alternate path for electricity to flow from the battery to the bulb. Electricity takes the easiest path. The light will shine as if the resistor did not exist.

Wrap the test lead loosely around the bulb assembly. Tuck any surplus lead wire under the lead itself. Then reassemble the light with the test lead inside. *Voila!* Bright mode. And if we remove the test lead? *Voila!* Energy-saver mode.

Is There Any Competition?

• **LED replacement bulbs.** LED flashlight bulbs are available that can replace incandescent bulbs. (Please know that "LED" covers a lot of ground. Some LED's are much more efficient than others.)

Both Rayovac and Dorcy sell LED upgrade bulbs for 2-cell flashlights. See below. **Given Heavy Duty batteries, the Dorcy LED bulb in a two-cell flashlight ran brighter than a new Solitaire for 50 hours.** Please recall that, with an incandescent bulb and Heavy Duty batteries, the old family flashlight only lasted *eight* hours.

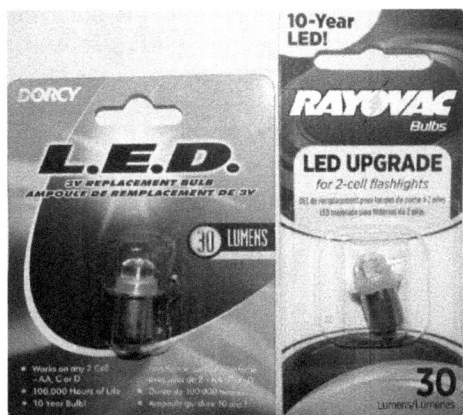

Additionally, Ozark Trail makes a table lamp for camping that comes with a regular, incandescent bulb and uses four D-cells (each 1.5 volts). **With a 6-volt Rayovac LED upgrade bulb and Duracell alkaline batteries, the Ozark Trail table lamp was brighter than a new Solitaire (in candle mode) for 360 hours.**

We must conclude that LED bulbs significantly increase a light's run time. On the other hand, 50 hours or even 360 hours poses no challenge to the 2000-hour flashlight.

Caution. Rayovac sells an extensive line of flashlight bulbs but only a couple are LED. Be sure the package specifies LED and that the bulb end is round, not pointy. The picture below shows an incandescent bulb on the left and an LED on the right. The selection can be confusing and it's easy to return home from shopping with the wrong thing.

• **Life+Gear.** It would be nice to buy a long-life flashlight straight off the shelf. So when I saw a Life+Gear flashlight, touted as running 300 hours, I bought one. It had four operating modes: (1) steady white, (2) steady white plus steady red, (3) steady red, and (4) flashing red. I was dismayed to get it home, read the fine print, and discover that the 300 hours applied only to the flashing red mode. Try reading the Bible with that.

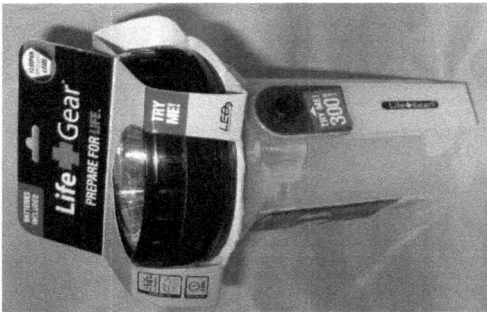

It was doubly annoying to discover "all functions turn off in 1 hour." So to get my 300 red-flashing hours, I'd have to turn the flashlight back on 299 times. And everything really did shut down after one hour of operation. Fortunately, Walmart was kind enough to refund my $14.88.

• **Pak-Lite.** Pak-Lite (www.9voltlight.com/home) sells LED flashlights that run on square 9-volt batteries (the kind that powered 6-transister radios back in the day). Pak-Lite prices range from $11.99 for the basic model to $32.99 for the "Ultra."

Blocklite, $9.90 at Amazon, is another 9-volt brand. Energizer sells rechargeable 9-volt dry cells.

I bought a Pak-Lite Ultra because it came with a lithium battery promising extended run times. The Ultra has a bright mode (80+ hours of run time) and a "soft" mode (1200+ hours). These long run times require a lithium battery. Replacement lithium batteries are $7.99 from Rayovac.

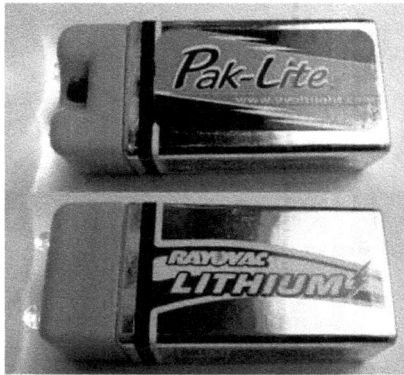

Pak-Lite does not provide any lumen ratings but I found the Pak-Lite on bright mode to be brighter than a new Solitaire. Unfortunately, the advertised 80+ hours of run time is awfully distant from what the 2000-hour flashlight will do. Because the two numbers (80 vs. 2000) were so far apart, I couldn't bring myself to ruin an $8 battery to establish the exact number — 80 hours, 90 hours, or whatever.

On soft mode, Pak-Lite output was less than 10% (by my estimate) the brightness of a Solitaire. So for comparison to a Solitaire, Pak-Lite soft-mode didn't qualify for the race; it failed before it started.

Blocklite also has "high" and "low" modes of operation but is silent on run time and lumens.

These little lights are undeniably handy because of their small size but for sheer run time they're not in the same league with a 150-ohm resistor in a 5109LS. How could they be? A little 9-volt battery only weighs 1.5 ounces. An alkaline 6-volt weighs two pounds. As far as available juice is concerned, it's like comparing a nickel and a dollar.

Bottom Line

Years ago, I worked with an equipment salesman who had a big poster over his desk. It read: "CHEAP — FAST — GOOD. Pick any two." I've often smiled at the truth in that poster.

• CHEAP. The 2000-hour flashlight is a $5 light with a 30-cent resistor. It's cheap.

• FAST. The parts are easy to find. Lowe's and Home Depot and Kmart all carry the light. Radio Shack sells the resistor. The "hack" or modification is a half-hour job. It's fast.

• GOOD. It will output a useful amount of light, continuously, around the clock, for 2000 hours. It's good.

"CHEAP — FAST — GOOD. Pick any two." The 2000-hour flashlight is perhaps the only item I've ever seen where you can pick all three.

APPENDIX I: Where Can I Get Parts?

Flashlight

The flashlight used in this hack is an Eveready 5109LS. It comes with a battery strapped to its bottom. For reasons unknown, Eveready keeps the model number semi-secret. It appears in small print on the plastic wrapping.

Lowe's and Home Depot both stock these lights in their brick-and-mortar stores for $4.97. Between the US, Canada, and Mexico, Lowe's has 1,745 stores; Home Depot, 2,252. If you look online, Lowe's lists this light as model 5109LSH7 and Home Depot as 5109LSH15. When you get one in your hands, the model number is 5109LS. I've also seen the 5109LS at Walgreens and Kmart.

Online, it appears that everyone except Lowe's and Home Depot calls it a 5109LS. If you do buy online, you'll have to pay shipping. It's available from several sources (Amazon, Office Depot, Best Buy, Advance Auto Parts, Auto Zone, Pep Boys Online, PlumberSurplus.com, Ace Hardware, eBay, etc.). Including shipping, it will cost you somewhere between $9 and $20. Quite a spread for the same light.

Walmart doesn't carry it in their U.S. stores (at least the branches I checked) but you can order online from Walmart and pick it up at one of their retail stores. There's no shipping charge but the price is $10.24.

In Toronto, Canada, I was surprised to find that Lowe's did not carry the 5109LS in stock. I was even more surprised to find that Walmart did. That's exactly the opposite of what I found in the states. Go figure.

കൗയ്യ ഉൗയ്യ

Now here's an unexpected wrinkle. In May 2013 I discovered first Kmart and then Lowe's (U.S.) selling a 5109LS **10X** flashlight side by side with a 5109LS **5X**. Same make and model, same price, different label. The 10X version claimed 130 hours of run time whereas the 5X version claimed 65 hours.

To all outward appearances (other than the label) the two lights were the same. The 10X label was copyrighted 2012; the 5X label was copyrighted 2010. So what's going on here? I bought a 10X, took it home, and tested it.

Given a Heavy Duty battery and no resistor added, for the first 150 hours the stock flashlight labeled 10X was brighter than a new Solitaire. For the next 25 hours it was equal. After that, it gave less light than a new Solitaire.

The 10X results were thus not as good as the outcome reported earlier for the 5X (see "Test Results" above). I was surprised. I expected the 10X to be at least equal to the 5X but it was worse.

Statistically, the observed variation can be chalked up to small sample size. With the 10X light I happened to get a poor battery. Or, the 5X came with a better-than-average battery. Either way, it was luck of the draw. It's fair to conclude that the flashlights are the same; the labels are different.

If you find yourself shaking your head and muttering, "No way; there's gotta be more to it than that," then I urge you to buy a 5X and a 10X yourself and compare them side by side. The combined price of both lights, including batteries, is only ten bucks. Seeing the results with your own eyes will save a lot of brouhaha.

Resistors

The resistor shown in the Bill of Material, earlier, is from Radio Shack; they have has 4,476 U.S. stores.

You will find local hobbyist and electronics stores in many areas (Radio Shack competitors) who also carry resistors. NTE is one brand (from NTE Electronics, Inc., 44 Farrand Street, Bloomfield, NJ 07003). A local hobby store in my area charges $1.25 for a pack of six NTE resistors.

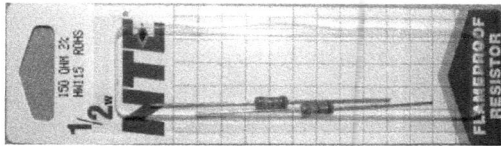

A word of caution about buying resistors. When you go to Radio Shack and ask for a resistor, the clerk will guide you to a cabinet containing hundreds of neatly labeled packets. He will then abandon you to wait on someone else.

Let's say you want a 150-ohm resistor. Be careful that the package says "150" and not "150k." Lowercase k stands for kilo (meaning thousand). And you want a 150-ohm resistor, not a 150,000-ohm resistor.

It's worse online. There you will find resistors with ratings from picoohms (a trillionth of an ohm) to teraohms (a trillion ohms). But you want **ohms**, *something with no prefix or suffix.*

Conductive Wire Glue

A tube of wire glue from Radio Shack is shown under the Bill of Materials, above.

You can also find wire glue on eBay (see below). It costs about $10, postage included, for 0.3 fluid oz. It is item # 0400 from Anders Div. of Idolon Tech., 72 Stone Place, Melrose, MA 02176.

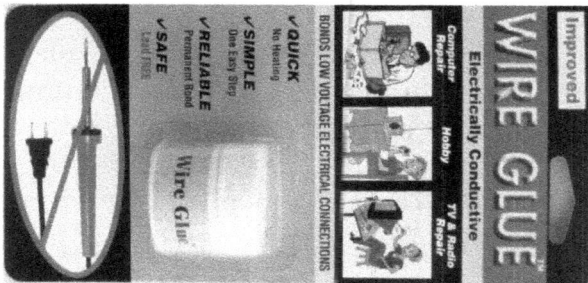

APPENDIX II: Using AAA, AA, C, and D-Cells.

• **D-CELLS.** With the help of some adapters, battery sizes other than a square 6-volt dry cell can be used. D-cells are the easiest because Rayovac sells a readymade adapter.

I checked out the run time of a 5109LS with a 150-ohm resistor and rechargeable D-cells. **For the first 200 hours, this configuration was brighter than the Solitaire.**

The batteries were brand new Energizer NiMH's, rated at 2500 mAh (2500 milli-amp-hours), charged for 16.5 hours on an Energizer-brand charger.

Compared to 6-volt dry-cell results, 200 hours might not sound like much. On the contrary, it shows just how thrifty is the 2000-hour flashlight with whatever juice is provided to it.

Rechargeable Energizer D-cells in a traditional two-cell flashlight (with an incandescent bulb) will only last six hours. At eight hours the flashlight will be flat-out dead. So to squeeze 200 hours of useable light out of these puppies looks like bragging rights to me.

- **AA's.** Next, let's look at AA's.

This Appendix is perhaps more "advanced" than previous sections because it assumes you understand basic terms like volts, amps, watts, wiring in series and parallel, etc. I'm reluctant to explain these terms as we go along because it would drag out the presentation plus convert this how-to manual into an eighth-grade science primer on electronics.

I have a little camp light or table lamp, call it what you will, that holds four AA batteries. I put in four new Heavy Duty batteries. A mere $2^1/_2$ hours later I discovered the lamp was flat-out dead; the batteries totally consumed. **In contrast, the 2000-hour flashlight with four AA's (taken from the same package) was brighter than a new Solitaire for 100 hours.** A hundred hours instead of two? Can I get an "Amen brother" on that?

At Radio Shack, as well as other electronics stores, you can buy "battery holders." The common battery sizes (AAA, AA, C, and D) are all 1.5 volts. If wired in series, nose to tail, four 1.5-volt batteries will produce 6 volts – exactly what the 2000-hour flashlight requires.

Safety Note. *Don't mix battery sizes (AA's with AAA's) or types (Heavy Duty with alkaline) or charge condition (one run-down battery with three new batteries). Why? Heat generation. Like water seeking its own level, current rushes to the weakest battery. The flow is not regulated. The weak battery gets hot. Fires can and do happen. But there's no reason for it if we use common sense and a bit of caution.*

Let's look at the AA battery holder first. After that, we'll see how the flashlight must be modified. The light modification is very simple. Well, OK, crude.

Above we see a 4-pack battery holder for AA's. The Radio Shack part number is 2700409. The red wire is positive. I cut a red test lead (the kind with an alligator clip on each end) in half, stripped some insulation from the cut end, soldered the wire from the battery pack to the test lead, and covered the splice with heat shrink tubing. I repeated the splicing on the black side. To avoid confusion in an emergency situation, I labeled with adhesive tape the wire that goes to the center.

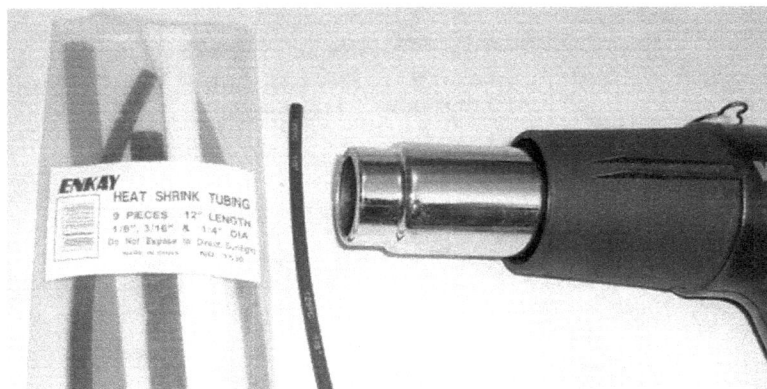

I used a heat gun for the "heat shrink tubing" but a hair dryer will also work. If pressed, you can simply twist the wire ends together and cover the splice with plastic electrician's tape.

• **AAA's.** The same kind of 4-pack battery holder is available for AAA's. The Radio Shack part number for the AAA holder is 2700411.

• **C-CELLS.** The best C-cell holder I found was branded Philmore, part number BH243, from LKG Industries, 3660 Publishers Drive, Rockford, IL 61109. It's open-faced, rather than closed, so a wrap of tape should be used to hold the batteries in place. Even when taped, if you drop the flashlight, a battery may pop loose. (Ask me how I know.)

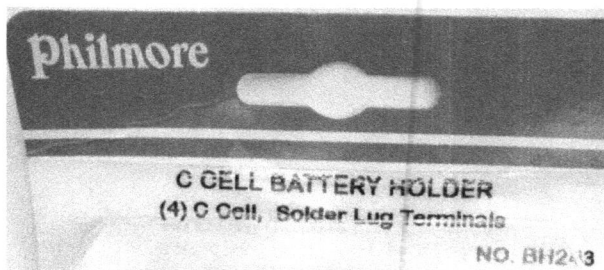

• **PREPARING THE FLASHLIGHT.** Now we can prepare the flashlight. When complete, the wiring hookup looks like this:

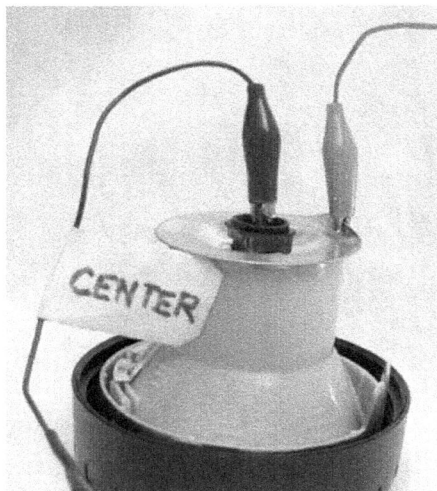

We've forced-fit a small screw into the center of the bulb assembly so as to clip the negative alligator to it. And, with a pair of pliers, we've bent the flat metal ring so as to receive the red/positive alligator. I warned you it was crude.

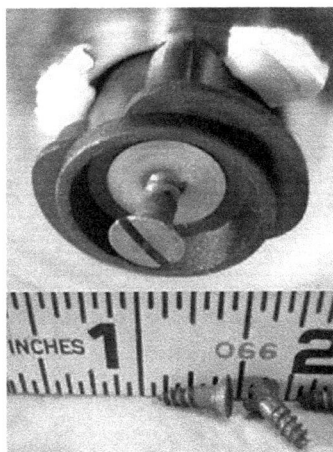

Now we can lower the battery pack into the body of the flashlight (where the big 6-volt dry cell normally resides), clip our alligators to the appropriate terminals, and we're in business. *Let there be light!* Hark! What's that I hear?

Halleluiah! Halleluiah! Hallay-lu-yaah!

APPENDIX III: Some Shameless Self-Promotion.

Hi. I'm Ron Brown, author of this manual, *The Amazing 2000-Hour Flashlight*. I want to tell you a little about myself plus explain the bonus I've included here. (It's the next Appendix.)

I published my first magazine article in 1982. They paid me $300. Over the next two years I published several more articles. The topics were shop tips and small-scale farming. I was quite pleased with myself one day to discover two different magazines simultaneously on the same newsstand, each with national circulation and each carrying one of my stories.

But the articles took time to research. And I was raising a family. Plus the magazines themselves didn't really pay that much. (They didn't have to. Writing is competitive. There are lots of smart people with good writing skills who would give their stuff away for the honor of being published.) It forced me out of the game.

A bit later, in 1987, I placed a book on firearms with Loompanics Unlimited. In their catalog, Loompanics billed my book as "the single finest book of its type ever written." Loompanics is gone now, but at least I can say I sold a paper-and-ink book to a royalty publisher. Today, in this ebook era, not too many people can make that claim.

In the 1990's I self-published a book on personal finance (again, paper-and-ink). It covered stock-picking and portfolio strategy as well as money creation and banking.

One reader said it was the first time in years he'd stayed up all night and read a book, cover to cover, in one sitting. Another reader was even more flattering; he bought four additional copies as gifts.

The end of that project came with a phone call from my son. "Dad, how many copies of that finance book do you have left?"

"About 400. Not sure exactly."

"So 400 books at $20 each would be $8000, right?"

"Yeah."

"I'll take 'em."

"*What?* What are you gonna do with 'em."

"Burn 'em."

"***WHAT?***" I don't know about you, but I've never been real big into book burning.

"Dad, you're giving this stuff away. Just tell me you won't have any more printed and I'll buy your entire inventory."

Well, I didn't sell him the books. But his call got the wheels turning in my head and a couple of months later I pulled it off the market and shut down the Web page.

In 2002 I retired. As in collecting-Social-Security retired. The following year, out of the blue, I received a job offer in Canada. I started work August 1, 2003. The lights went out exactly two weeks later. The Northeast was dark for days.

The company had put us up in a luxury townhouse. Chandeliers, pool, maid service, all that stuff.

But what good was it? We had no lights, no way to cook, no refrigeration. As raw newcomers we had no friends or family . . . no TV . . . no radio . . . no local currency to speak of. And the stores were all closed anyway because the cash registers didn't work.

When the sun went down it was bedtime. We did have some fancy candlesticks on the mantle. They were a blessing. Though some candles would have been nice.

Only later did I learn how close my wife had been to begging me, "Let's go home. I'm scared. I don't care about the job. I don't care about the money. Let's get the hell out of here."

Fear of the dark coupled with fear of the unknown is a powerful force.

So a couple of years later I retired for real and began researching *Lanterns, Lamps & Candles: A User's Guide.* Shortly after publication, I queried readers as to how they liked it. My question was, "How would you rate it on a scale from one to ten?"

The very first response said this: "Honestly, it's a 10+. Nothing else comes close. LOVED it."

And that brings us to the bonus included here as the next Appendix: Chapter One of *Lanterns, Lamps & Candles*. It will hopefully pique your curiosity and cause you to wonder, "What else is lurking around that I probably should know and probably don't?"

Which means you'll have to buy the CD and get your hands on the other nineteen chapters, yes? And wouldn't it be great to buy four additional copies as gifts? I think so.

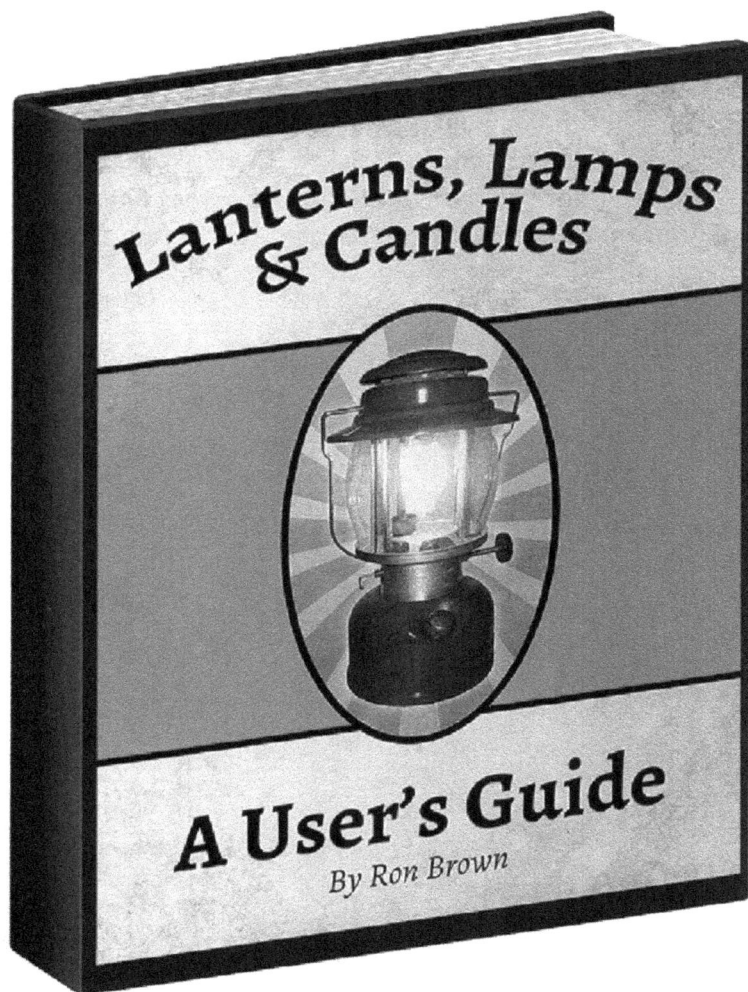

Copyright © 2012 Ronald B. Brown
http://www.rc-publishing.com/

Chapter One
Matches and Lighters

This chapter was inspired by the following Internet dialogue (I'm paraphrasing):

"I've inherited an old Zippo cigarette lighter from my grandfather. Can I use charcoal lighter fluid in it?"

Well, why not? There's Zippo (brand name) *lighter fluid*. And Ronsonol (brand name) *lighter fluid*. And charcoal *lighter fluid*:

It's like a discussion with my wife about cheese balls. To me, a cheese ball is made from semi-soft cheese, is the size of a baseball, and is rolled in crushed nutmeats.

To her, cheese balls are the size of marbles, made of puffy cheese-curl stuff, and contain orange dye that sticks to your teeth. Both are popular at parties.

Turns out there are different things named cheese balls. There are different things named lighter fluid.

****

Bad Info

The Internet question – "Can I use charcoal lighter fluid in my Zippo?" – received an Internet answer: "If you fill a Zippo with charcoal lighter fluid, you can kiss your eyebrows and nose hairs goodbye. And any other part of your anatomy that's close to the explosion when it occurs."

That answer is 100% wrong. It was followed immediately by a second 100% wrong answer: "Charcoal lighter fluid in a Zippo? No way. You must use butane."

And a response: "Well, I finally got my Zippo apart but I still can't figure out how to put in the butane."

● "The difference between stupidity and genius is that genius has its limits." – *Albert Einstein*

****

Let's deal first with the Zippo/butane thing.

Zippo (brand) lighters were patented in 1936 and saw their heyday with the GI's of World War II. Zippos used liquid fuel (white gas). The tiny fuel tank was stuffed with cotton fluff so that the liquid didn't spill into your pocket. A wick brought the fuel to the flame by capillary action.

■ *Refilling a Zippo. First pull the innards out of the case. Then turn the inner assembly upside down and lift the felt retainer. Insert the spout of the fluid can and squeeze. The juice flows out of the can and into the cotton fluff inside the lighter. The fluid can is simply a can. It is not pressurized like a butane canister.* ■

Zippo's reign as king of the lighters ended in 1973 when Bic introduced disposable butane lighters that could provide 3,000 lights before wearing out. How do you spell, "Goodbye Zippo"? **ANSWER:** "Flick my Bic."

Today, a new Zippo costs $13 and a small can of fuel, $2.75. Or, you can buy a package of five butane lighters (Bic knock-offs, pre-filled with fuel) for one buck at the Dollar Store. One Zippo and a can of fuel equals 78 butane lighters.

Judging by the Internet, people born after 1970 may have never seen a Zippo-style lighter. They sincerely believe that butane is the one and only fuel ever used in cigarette lighters.

So we need to understand butane a little better:

■ **LEFT to RIGHT:** *(1) disposable butane lighter; (2) refillable butane lighter; (3) to fill, hold both canister and lighter upside down, mate the fittings, push until it feels good.* ■

Water boils and turns from a liquid to a gas at 212° F. Butane boils and turns from a liquid to a gas at 31° F. Just about the time ice is melting, butane is boiling. That's why it's a gas at room temperature. In a refill canister, butane is a liquid only by merit of the fact that it's been put under pressure, not unlike an aerosol spray can.

You can get the butane out of its canister by (1) turning it upside down, (2) holding it at a slight angle, and (3) pressing the injecting needle onto a hard surface. The butane comes out as a liquid but you can actually see it bubbling as it boils away. It will volatilize into the atmosphere far too quickly to be of any use in your Zippo. (And you won't like the way it smells either.)

****

Okay. We're finally ready to talk about charcoal lighter fluid (also known as mineral spirits). If you remember, that was the original question.

Can you substitute charcoal lighter fluid for Zippo/Ronsonol lighter fluid? And the answer came back, "No! It will explode."

Wrong! But where does the idea come from that charcoal lighter fluid is explosive?

IT STARTS HERE: In an effort to hurry things along, charcoal lighter fluid is sometimes sprayed on a charcoal grill that is already burning. (Let us be clear here. We're talking about a charcoal *grill*, not a gas *grill*.)

The lighter fluid doesn't break into open flame because the burning charcoal itself only glows; no flame exists to ignite the fluid. (And ignition does require a flame or a spark. Don't you remember dowsing your cigarette in a cup of gasoline to impress the girls?)

But, although no ignition takes place, the fluid gets hot. It begins to vaporize and smoke. It goes above its "flash point" but there's still no flame to set it off. When it reaches its "autoignition temperature" (i.e. 473 $^\circ$F where a flame is no longer required) – **POOF!**

The flameless preheating vaporizes a large quantity of liquid before ignition occurs. And that's the problem. Half a teaspoon is not a threat to your eyebrows. Half a cup is a threat to your house. Flameless preheating does not get proper credit for the results.

No "explosion" can occur as long as mineral spirits remains at room temperature. At room temperature, mineral spirits is a liquid. And a liquid must vaporize and turn to gas before it can oxidize . . . that is, combine with oxygen . . . that is, burn.

This is 9th grade science.

SIDE NOTE: To those not familiar with the term, "mineral spirits" sounds like it's plural. It's not. Mineral spirits is singular. It does take some getting used to.

****

Zippo lighter fluid is highly volatile. Technically it is flammable. It readily evaporates. At room temperature, vapors are always present that can be ignited with a flame or even a spark.

For all practical purposes, charcoal lighter fluid does not evaporate at room temperature and is termed combustible. Vapors are too few and far between to catch fire. Like candle wax, it must be preheated to the point of forming a vapor before ignition can take place. A match performs the preheating function as well as the ignition-of-vapors function.

As fuel in a Zippo, charcoal lighter fluid (like motor oil) will not work. Spinning the striker wheel will create a shower of sparks but the sparks won't produce enough heat to vaporize the fuel. The lighter will not light, much less explode. Your nose hairs are safe.

Zippo Fuel Substitutes

But this brings up an interesting possibility. Although we can't use combustible liquids (diesel fuel, kerosene, mineral spirits) in a Zippo, can we substitute other flammable liquids (gasoline, Coleman fuel, acetone)? Will they work?

"Flammability" and "combustibility" are defined in Chapter Six.

- Let's start at ground zero. Zippo and/or Ronsonol lighter fluid. Do they work in a Zippo-style cigarette lighter? Yes.
- Coleman fuel. Does it work in a Zippo lighter? Yes. White gas with a dash of perfume equals cigarette lighter fluid. (Note that Coleman fuel sells for $10 per gallon whereas Zippo lighter fluid sells for $88 per gallon when purchased in 4 oz. cans.)
- Other flammable liquids – gasoline (petrol), lacquer thinner, acetone – do they work? No. At least not the way I'd hoped.

The problem is the Zippo wick. Perhaps it is too small in diameter. Or too big. Or too dense. Or too fluffy. Or the wrong material (Zippo wicks are asbestos). After all, it was engineered to lift one specific fuel, white gas, from the fuel tank to the flame. Acetone was not a consideration.

BUT if you put two drops of acetone (or other flammable liquid; see below) directly on the wick of a Zippo and spin the striker wheel, the acetone will ignite and burn for 30 seconds. And thirty seconds of live flame is not bad. Plenty of time to light a twist of paper or splinter of wood which can then be used to light your candle or your campfire.

Some common flammable liquids:

- VM&P naphtha (i.e. varnish makers' and painters' naphtha; naphtha is an alternate name for white gas).

- Gasoline (petrol to the Brits).
- Acetone (nail polish remover).
- Lacquer thinner.
- Denatured alcohol (used as shellac thinner and as fuel in marine   stoves).
- Dry gas (methanol).

CAUTION: *Alcohol flames are hard to see.*

IMCO Lighters

There's an English chap on eBay selling IMCO lighters. Developed in the 1930's, they're made in Austria and appear to be Europe's answer to the Zippo. From the eBay sales pitch:

> *"These lighters are a great piece of kit, they are more user friendly than a Zippo, cheaper and double up as a candle . . . Runs on Lighter fluid or Petrol . . . IMCO has produced and sold over HALF A BILLION (yes half a billion!!) lighters."*

In the interest of completeness for this book, I bought one (for £6.95 including postage). What intrigued me was the possibility of multi-fuel use. And, indeed, with its cotton wick, it operates on gasoline (petrol) very nicely.

****

Bad Info

Unfortunately, someone might believe that these lighters "double up as a candle."

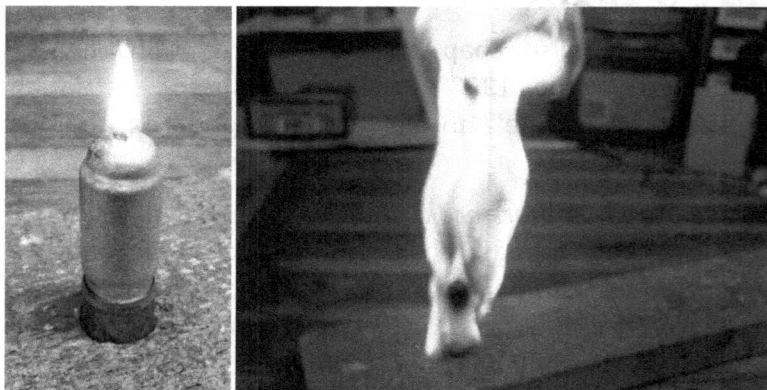

■ **LEFT:** *The set-up. I inserted the IMCO "candle" in a $^5/_8$"* *diameter hole so it wouldn't get knocked over.* **RIGHT:** *This happened suddenly at 15 minutes. Sorry the focus is poor; it caught me off guard.* ■

****

MATCHES

There are two kinds of matches safety and strike anywhere. Safety matches won't accidentally ignite in your pocket whereas strike anywhere matches can and sometimes do. Safety matches are also called strike-on-box.

There are three sizes: paper matches (called book matches); small wooden matches (called penny matches); and large wooden kitchen matches.

More than you ever wanted to know about match chemistry:

The head of a strike anywhere match is a progressive "explosive train." A tiny bit of primary explosive is detonated. That ignites the main body of the match head. That in turn ignites the paraffin wax (with which the first half inch of the wooden matchstick is impregnated). The burning paraffin in turn ignites the wooden stick.

The very tip of a strike anywhere match contains potassium chlorate plus phosphorus sesquisulfide (a.k.a. tetraphosphorus trisulfide, trisulfurated phosphorus, and phosphorus sulfide). It's is a primary explosive, sensitive to friction, impact, and heat.

If you cut off the tiny white tip of a strike anywhere match, place it on an anvil, and rap it with a hammer, it will sound like a .22 rimfire rifle cartridge (almost).

It was once a test of manhood for teenage boys to light their cigarettes from strike anywhere matches — matches that they lit one-handed, using their thumbnail as the striker. If a chunk of burning match head got lodged under one's thumbnail, of course, it could ruin an otherwise pleasant afternoon. Trust me on this.

Safety matches (strike-on-box) contain potassium chlorate plus sulfur in the match head and red phosphorus in the gritty striking surface printed on the matchbook or matchbox.

The act of striking produces friction and heat. The heat converts a tiny amount of red phosphorous into white phosphorous vapor which ignites spontaneously. This heat decomposes the potassium chlorate, liberating oxygen, and causes the sulfur to burn. This in turn ignites the wood or paper body of the match.

Where can I buy strike anywhere matches?

In the USA, strike anywhere matches virtually disappeared from store shelves for twenty years – a generation. The old-time brands were Ohio Blue Tip and Diamond. Today, Diamond owns Ohio Blue Tip. But, regardless of brand, the question, "Where can I buy strike anywhere matches?" appeared year after year on Internet forums.

The only place I knew for sure was Canada. The Redbird brand, manufactured by the Eddy Match Co., was (and still is) sold by No Frills (a large grocery chain) and Canadian Tire (in the camping section). The price is $1.25 per box of 250.

But strike anywhere matches are making a comeback. Today, Diamond-brand strike anywhere matches (eco-friendly with green and white tips) can be purchased on eBay for about $4 per box of 300 including postage. They arrive in an envelope marked USPS FIRST-CLASS™ PKG.

I still haven't seen them face-to-face in the big-box stores (e.g. Wal-Mart, Target) so I was slightly amazed to find them just the other day in my local Mom-and-Pop grocery store. One U.S. dollar per box of 300. Strike anywhere matches are once again appearing on store shelves.

****

Bad Info

While they were on hiatus, one story had it that strike anywhere matches were classified as HazMat (hazardous material) and incurred excessive transportation costs. Consumers were not willing to pay the higher price and, for that reason, retailers didn't stock them. But, as far as I know, safety matches were also classified HazMat.

Another story had it that chemicals in the strike anywhere tips were used in homebrew crystal meth recipes. Wrong again. If anything, it was the red phosphorous in the striker panel that was of interest, nothing in the match head.

****

Waterproof Matches

I decided to test some homegrown methods of waterproofing against commercial matches. The tests consisted of "waterproofing" ordinary strike anywhere matches (dipping in paraffin wax, painting with shellac, etc., whatever recipes I could find), letting them dry 24 hours, then soaking them – side-by-side with commercial waterproof matches – in a bucket of water overnight.

I was astonished to find that the commercial waterproof matches (Coghlan's, Stansport, Coleman's, and UCO Stormproof; with prices ranging from 1¢ to 12¢ per match) didn't work. The heads were all mushy and crumbled when striking. They might have been water resistant but none of them were waterproof. Ditto for the homegrown methods.

No doubt my surprise resulted from my expectations. I expect a plastic poncho to be waterproof. I expect rubber boots to be waterproof. I expect a bulletproof vest to be bulletproof. "Here. Put on this bullet-resistant vest and let's go capture the bank robbers." Yeah, right.

Nail polish came the closest of anything to working but the matches were no longer "strike anywhere." Strike some places would be a better description. Matchbox, yes. Side of carborundum grinding wheel, yes. Sandpaper and rocks, maybe.

And the entire match had to be painted with nail polish. If only the head-end were coated, water penetrated the exposed wood, traveled the length of the stick, and turned the match head mushy.

Conclusion:

A mechanical container remains the only for-sure way I know to have a dry match when you need it. One buck. Cheap.

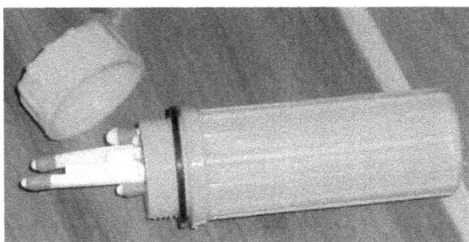

****

excerpted from *Lanterns, Lamps & Candles: A User's Guide*
for sale at http://www.rc-publishing.com/

APPENDIX V: Free Bonus Chapter from Gaye Levy

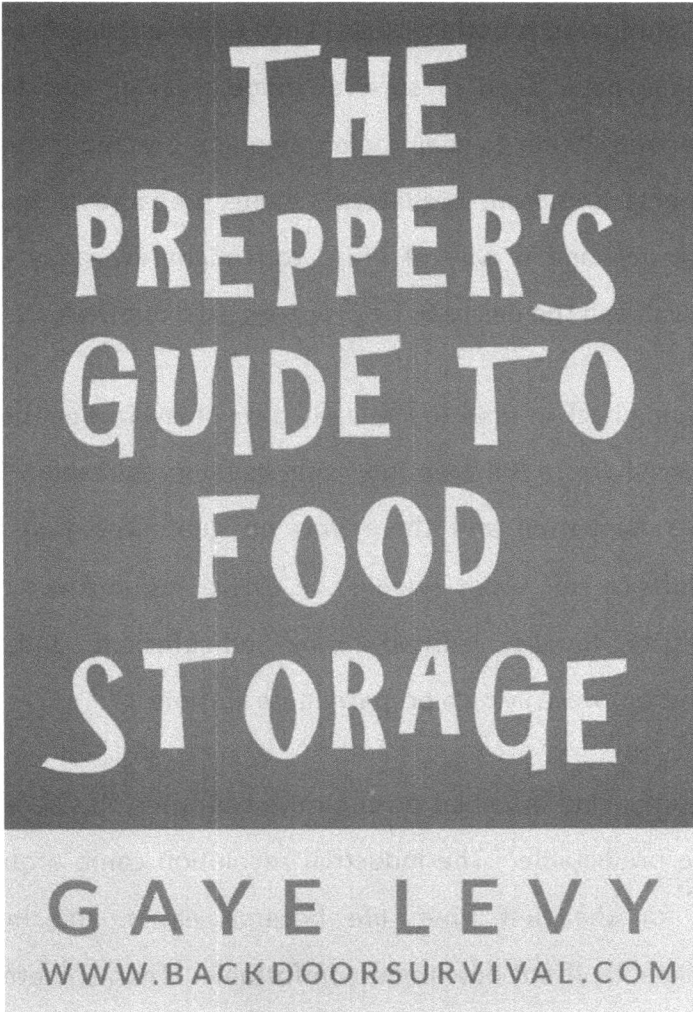

THE PREPPER'S GUIDE TO FOOD STORAGE

GAYE LEVY

WWW.BACKDOORSURVIVAL.COM

Food for the Preparedness Pantry

Being prepared is nothing new. Since the beginning of time, humans have been in survival mode, seeking out food, water and shelter to keep them safe and protected from the elements and from predators. Being prepared is simply instinctive and a way of life. You might even say that survival, and the desire to be prepared, is in our DNA.

Stepping back in time to the early days of civilization, being prepared was a full time job. Life was unpredictable. Bad things happened and there was no guarantee that the abundance of today would be there tomorrow. By necessity, families learned to be self-sufficient, and, by definition, were living a preparedness lifestyle.

As humankind marched through the centuries, life became more predictable. The industrial revolution came around, and for the first time, life became easier and more predictable, if not downright comfortable. Then something happened.

Just after the dawn of the 21st century, terrorists attacked the United States, jeopardizing the sense of security not only for its citizens but all citizens o/f the western world. Massive storms and tsunamis destroyed homes and businesses throughout the planet resulting in death and destruction. Likewise, economies throughout the world faltered resulting in unemployment, the loss of homes and financial uncertainty.

For many, the predictable and comfortable lifestyle became tenuous and elusive. Ordinary citizens became frightened, scared, fearful, and worried about an uncertain future. They knew they needed to do something to become better prepared for uncertainties and disasters, but what and how? Where should they start? And how do they do so while maintaining at least some semblance of their comfortable lifestyle?

While these are all important questions, many are beyond the scope of this particular book. Instead, *The Prepper's Guide to Food Storage* tackles a question that is foremost on everyone's mind: ***What will I eat?***

In these pages I will answer this question. This is a book about food: what to store, how to store and best practices.

It is a roadmap for showing ordinary citizens that long-term food storage is not something that will overwhelm you and not something that will burden your family or the family budget. It is based upon my own tried and true personal experience as someone who has learned to live the preparedness lifestyle by approaching emergency preparation and planning in a systematic, step-by-step manner.

Why Food?

When most people start thinking about preparedness, they focus on food. Not shelter, gear, sanitation, power, self-defense or the myriad of other concerns that need to be addressed following an emergency or disaster situation. Quite simply, food is the number one concern people have second only to their concern for having an adequate supply of water.

What type of food should you buy, where should you buy it, and how should you store it? You are going to learn that acquiring food for the preparedness pantry does not have to be overwhelming. Furthermore, long-term emergency food storage it is something you can do over the course of a week, a month, or even longer, if that is what it takes.

Perhaps even more important, when done filling your storage pantry, you will be secure in the knowledge that if a disaster strikes, you will have plenty of food to feed your family, along with a few treats and surprises along the way.

Store What You Eat and Eat What You Store

When most people first start thinking about emergency food storage, they have a vision of tasteless prepackaged foods that are highly processed, expensive and made up of unintelligible mystery ingredients. They also assume that emergency food is something you purchase then hide away in some obscure part of your home, never to see daylight again unless there is an emergency.

Although that is one approach to food storage, it is not the approach that I take and most certainly is not the approach that I am going to recommend for you. Instead, I am going to teach you how to build a real food storage pantry that is stocked with healthy foods that can be mixed and matched to create an array of tasty meals. These are foods that you already eat. They are familiar to you and you know how to use them.

This leads us to the most important rule of food storage: *store what you eat and eat what you store.*

So how do you do that? What to buy, how much to buy, where to buy it, how much to pay, and where to store it are all common questions that a prepper will eventually ask him or herself.

The Prepper's Guide to Food Storage by Gaye Levy will answer these questions and more, available as a Kindle eBook at http://www.amazon.com/dp/B00H8DGY5M

*M*odern times began in 1879 with Edison's light bulb.

And there's nothing like a blackout to show how dependent we've grown . . .

"Oops! The baby's coming! *Now!* Get me to the hospital. Go get the car out of the underground parking garage. Yeah, I know it's midnight and the grid is down and it's pitch black down there. Just get the car."

The Amazing 2000-Hour Flashlight, the book you have in your hands, will empower you; give you control; bring you peace of mind.

But even the best flashlights eventually fail. Then you'll need *Lanterns, Lamps & Candles* (also by Ron Brown), available at *http://www.rc-publishing.com* . Note the title specifies USERS, not COLLECTORS.

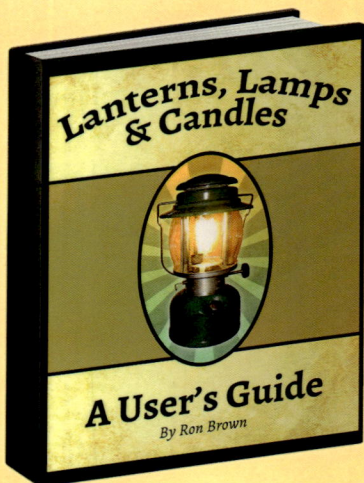

P.S. Great gift idea, too.

ISBN 9780985333720

90000

9 780985 333720

DEVOLUTION OF POWER

Rolling Back the Federal State to Preserve the Republic

William L. Kovacs